CHILDREN 92 ORTON 2012
Stone, Adam
Randy Orton

East Regional   04/10/2012

EAST REGIONAL

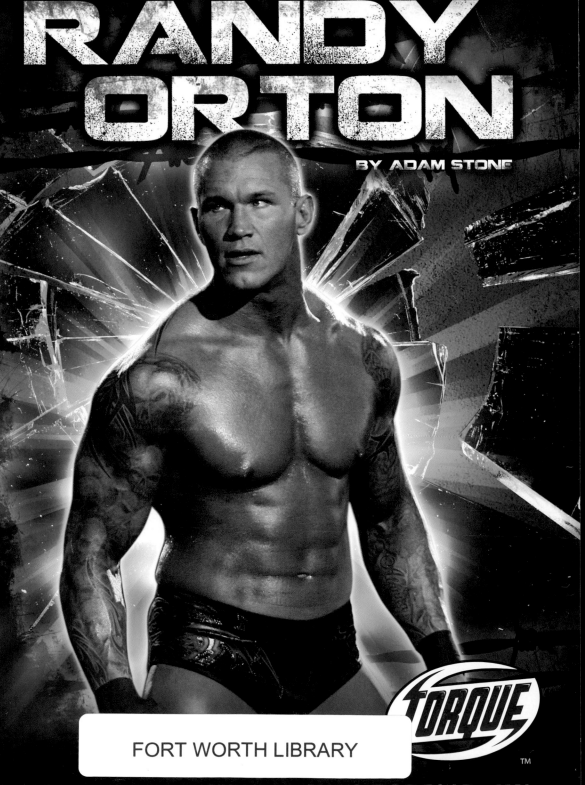

RANDY ORTON

BY ADAM STONE

FORT WORTH LIBRARY

TORQUE™

BELLWETHER MEDIA · MINNEAPOLIS, MN

Are you ready to take it to the extreme?
Torque books thrust you into the action-packed world
of sports, vehicles, mystery, and adventure. These books
may include dirt, smoke, fire, and dangerous stunts.
WARNING : read at your own risk.

Library of Congress Cataloging-in-Publication Data

Stone, Adam.
  Randy Orton / by Adam Stone.
     p. cm. -- (Torque: pro wrestling champions)
  Includes bibliographical references and index.
  Summary: "Engaging images accompany information about Randy Orton. The combination of
high-interest subject matter and light text is intended for students in grades 3 through 7"--Provided by
publisher.
  ISBN 978-1-60014-638-1 (hardcover : alk. paper)
  1. Orton, Randy--Juvenile literature. 2. Wrestlers--United States--Biography--Juvenile literature. I. Title.
  GV1196.O77S76 2011
  796.812092--dc22
  [B]   2011009106

This edition first published in 2012 by Bellwether Media, Inc.

Printed in the United States of America, North Mankato, MN.

CONTENTS

ROYAL RUMBLE

The action was intense at the 2009 **Royal Rumble**. Thirty wrestlers were competing to win the match. Randy Orton was the eighth wrestler to enter the ring. His friends Ted DiBiase and Cody Rhodes soon joined him. They worked with Orton to eliminate one wrestler after another.

VITAL STATS

Wrestling Name: _ _ _ _ _ _ _ _ _ _ _ _ Randy Orton

Real Name: _ _ _ _ _ _ _ _ _ _ _ Randal Keith Orton

Height: _ _ _ _ _ _ _ _ 6 feet, 4 inches (1.9 meters)

Weight: _ _ _ _ _ _ _ 245 pounds (111 kilograms)

Started Wrestling: _ _ _ _ _ _ _ _ _ _ _ _ _ _ _ 2000

Finishing Move: _ _ _ _ _ _ _ _ _ _ _ _ _ _ _ _ _ RKO

After a long battle, only Orton, DiBiase, Rhodes, and Triple H remained. Triple H tossed both DiBiase and Rhodes over the ropes. Then Orton smashed into Triple H from behind. Triple H sailed over the top rope. Randy Orton had won the Royal Rumble!

WHO IS RANDY ORTON?

Randal Keith Orton was born on April 1, 1980 in Knoxville, Tennessee. His father, "Cowboy" Bob Orton, was a professional wrestler. Orton watched his father wrestle legends like Hulk Hogan and "Rowdy" Roddy Piper.

Orton was on his high school wrestling team. His father didn't want him to be a professional wrestler. He told Orton that it was tough to spend a lot of time on the road.

QUICK HIT!

Orton's grandfather and uncle were also professional wrestlers. His grandfather wrestled as The Big O and his uncle as Barry O.

Orton graduated from high school in 1998. He joined the United States Marine Corps. While serving, Orton disobeyed orders from his officers. He also went **absent without leave (AWOL)** two times. He had to serve 38 days in a military prison. The Marine Corps gave him a **dishonorable discharge**.

Orton started training to become a professional wrestler after he left the military. In 2000, he wrestled in a small league and worked as a referee. World Wrestling Entertainment (WWE) signed him to a **developmental contract** in 2001. He wrestled for Ohio Valley Wrestling (OVW) as he prepared for the big stage.

QUICK HIT!

Orton won the OVW Hardcore Championship twice.

BECOMING A CHAMPION

Orton made his first television appearance for WWE in April 2002. He was a **face**, and the fans loved him. However, he hurt his shoulder and missed several months. Orton became a **heel** while he was injured. In 2003, Orton won the WWE Intercontinental Championship. He became a face again.

QUICK HIT!

Orton started calling himself "The Legend Killer." His goal was to wrestle and defeat the all-time greats of pro wrestling.

QUICK HIT!

Orton teamed up with Edge in 2006 to form Rated-RKO. The pair won the World Tag Team Championship that year.

Orton had become one of WWE's most popular wrestlers. In 2004, he beat Chris Benoit to win the World Heavyweight Championship. At age 24, he was the youngest heavyweight champion in WWE history. In 2007, Orton beat **rival** Triple H for the WWE Championship.

Orton is smaller than many WWE stars. He must be quick and have good **technique**. He has several **signature moves**. One is the dropkick. Orton jumps into the air and kicks both feet toward his opponent. He drives his feet into the opponent's chest. The knee drop is another favorite move. Orton performs it when his opponent is on the ground. He leaps into the air and drives his knee down into the opponent's chest.

KNEE
DROP

WRESTLE

Orton performs the **RKO** to end a match. This is his **finishing move**. Orton jumps into the air and grabs his opponent's head and neck. He twists his body as he falls. This slams the opponent's face into the mat. Difficult moves like the RKO have helped Orton follow in his father's footsteps. He is quickly becoming a WWE legend himself.

GLOSSARY

absent without leave (AWOL)—leaving a military post without permission

developmental contract—an agreement in which a wrestler signs with WWE but wrestles in a smaller league to gain experience and develop skills

dishonorable discharge—expulsion from the military for unacceptable behavior

face—a wrestler seen by fans as a hero

finishing move—a wrestling move meant to finish off an opponent so that he can be pinned

heel—a wrestler seen by fans as a villain

rival—a competitor with whom one is in a heated feud

RKO—Randy Orton's finishing move; Orton jumps at his opponent, wraps his arm around the opponent's head and neck, and brings the opponent's head down to the ground; the letters "RKO" are Orton's initials.

Royal Rumble—a popular WWE battle between 30 wrestlers; instead of starting all at once, wrestlers join the battle every few minutes.

signature moves—moves that a wrestler is famous for performing

technique—skillful and proper performance of moves

TO LEARN MORE

AT THE LIBRARY

Black, Jake. *The Ultimate Guide to WWE.* New York, N.Y.: Grosset & Dunlap, 2010.

Nemeth, Jason D. *Randy Orton.* Mankato, Minn.: Capstone Press, 2010.

Shields, Brian. *WWE Encyclopedia: The Definitive Guide to World Wrestling Entertainment.* New York, N.Y.: DK, 2009.

ON THE WEB

Learning more about Randy Orton is as easy as 1, 2, 3.

1. Go to www.factsurfer.com.

2. Enter "Randy Orton" into the search box.

3. Click the "Surf" button and you will see a list of related Web sites.

With factsurfer.com, finding more information is just a click away.

INDEX

The images in this book are reproduced through the courtesy of: Wire Image / Getty Images, front cover, pp. 12-13, 14-15, 16; Henry Wilson, p. 4; John Smolek, pp. 5, 6-7; Max Blain, pp. 8-9; David Seto, pp. 10-11, 17, 18-19; Devin Chen, pp. 20-21.